Learning Points

This simple, colourful book introduces young children to the idea of opposites. Illustrated in a lively, humorous style, opposites contains the words which describe relative sizes and positions, all shown through objects and scenes which will be familiar to young children.

- Encourage children to compare the sizes of their toys. Which is the biggest teddy? Which is the smallest? What is the largest marble they can find?

- Comparing family size is fun. Who is the tallest, the shortest? Who has the longest feet?

- Nursery rhymes are full of opportunities to focus on opposites: Humpty Dumpty, Jack and Jill, etc. Look out for these.

Ladybird books are widely available, but in case of difficulty may be ordered by post or telephone from:

Ladybird Books – Cash Sales Department
Littlegate Road Paignton Devon TQ3 3BE
Telephone 0803 554761

A catalogue record for this book is available from the British Library

Published by Ladybird Books Ltd Loughborough Leicestershire UK
Ladybird Books Inc Auburn Maine 04210 USA

Printed in EC

opposites

by HY MURDOCK
illustrated by TONY WELLS

Things have different shapes and sizes.

Some animals are **big**,
some animals are **little**.

Some people are **big**,
some are **middle-sized**
and some are **little**.

All around us
we see **large**
things and
small things.

Here are some more
shapes and sizes.

A **thin**
clown

A **fat** clown

A **tall** king

A **short** king

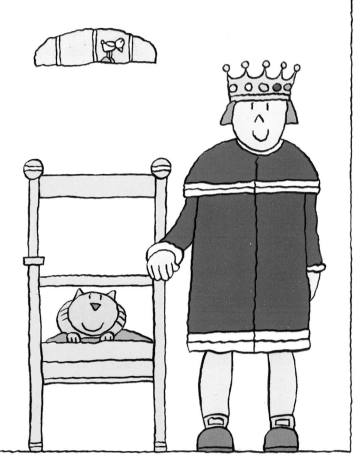

A **long** dragon

A **short** dragon

The boy rides
his bicycle
down the hill.

The man
pushes his bicycle
up the hill.

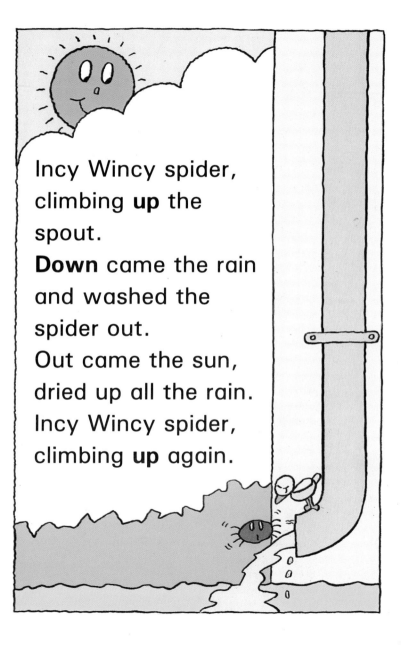

Incy Wincy spider,
climbing **up** the
spout.
Down came the rain
and washed the
spider out.
Out came the sun,
dried up all the rain.
Incy Wincy spider,
climbing **up** again.

We put our clothes **on** in
the morning.

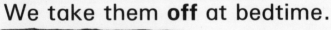

We take them **off** at bedtime.

The boy paints **high** up.

The girl paints **low** down.

The children play
indoors...

and **outdoors**.

Jack is **in** the box.

Jack is **out** of the box.